Code Making, Code Breaking

Contents

Written by Richard Platt
Illustrated by Robin Lawrie

What are codes and secret languages?

If you think only **spies** and soldiers use codes, you're wrong! We *all* use codes. They help us to address letters, talk on a phone, or even choose clothes.

Not all codes are secret. Some are easy ways to pass on facts quickly. For example, a postcode describes your street in six or seven letters and numbers. Anybody can find out what this code means.

Street names and road signs are codes too.

Secret codes are different. They have the opposite aim. They hide the meaning of a message. Secret codes are also called **ciphers**. Once a message is encoded (written in secret code), only someone who understands the code can read it.

Spies and soldiers have used secret codes to hide their plans almost since warfare began. But secret codes also keep all sorts of everyday things private. They hide your identity on the Internet and they even stop people listening in to your mobile phone calls.

code book used during the American Civil War (1861–5)

Part 1: Codes
Everyday codes
in life and art

Codes are everywhere around us. We see them all the time without really noticing them. Yet these simple signs make life easier to understand.

Have you ever walked down a street and seen colourful codes painted on the road and pavement? What do they mean? To find out, return in a few days. They'll be gone, and so will the piece of road they were on! These spray-can marks tell diggers where they need to repair a pipe or a cable that is buried under the road.

These coloured markings show that the road is about to be dug up by the water company (blue) and the electricity company (red). The white markings show where to dig or access the utilities.

Not all road markings are official. Nowadays, everyone wants free things. Busy people with portable computers look out for open wireless Internet hot spots. When they find one, they mark the pavement or wall. This is called "warchalking" and the markings even show how fast you can connect.

The things we wear can work as a kind of code. They send a message to people we meet. The clothes you choose can signal what football team you support, or which job you do.

It can be seen by the colours supporters are holding up that two different teams are being supported here – blue and white for Manchester City and red and white for Manchester United.

In the past, clothing codes spelt out names. Armoured knights of the **Middle Ages** wore special family signs, called arms, on shields and coats.

When a knight married, he and his bride joined their arms. Soon coats of arms became squared patterns of bright signs.

the coat of arms of a married couple

Since the Middle Ages, artists have used symbols, special signs, to put hidden messages in their paintings and sculptures. Animals, for example, stood for good or bad in humans. Bears stood for bad temper, bulls for brute force, crocodiles for deceit.

Painters used animals to show good and bad in humans. The dogs stand for faithfulness.

Ancient messages: smoke and fire

When a Greek army went to war around 3,200 years ago, it used a code to send news home. Mountain-top bonfires carried its message 600 kilometres. The flames signalled "victory", which meant "We beat the Trojans!"

Fires carry news fast. We see their bright glow by night and their smoke by day. However, fires send only simple signals: a lit fire could mean "victory" or "yes" and an unlit fire could mean "defeat" or "no".

Native American people used smoke for smarter messages. The Apache built three fires to signal "alarm!" Their families could see the three smoke **plumes** up to 80 kilometres away. Two fires signalled "We have made a camp." Just one meant "attention!"

In 1775, Americans fighting the British signalled with lantern flames. Their code was one light if troops advanced by land and two if they arrived by sea.

American silversmith Paul Revere spread news of the British advance in his midnight ride.

Naval flag signals and codes

Flapping on a high pole, a flag identifies a country –
or perhaps a company. Before the invention of
telephones or radios, flags did much more. Sailors used
them to send complete messages. Flag signals were
simple and quick. A special code meant just a few flags
could say a lot.

The signal flags had brightly coloured patterns.
At the top of a ship's mast, they were easy to tell apart.
There was a flag for each letter of the alphabet.
However, they rarely spelt out words. Instead, signallers
looked up what they wanted to say in a code book.
This listed words and names, with a two-, three- or
four-flag code for each. Just a few flag codes could save
spelling out a long sentence.

For example, this signal …

… stood for the letters HYF. In the sailors' code book,
the signal HYF meant "I am jammed fast on the rocks."

Place names all had four-flag codes, which saved a lot of spelling. For example:

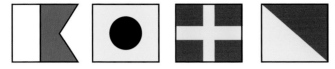

stood for the German town of Königswusterhausen.

The most urgent messages needed just one flag. On its own, the "K" flag meant "Stop sailing immediately!"

the K flag

Watching through a telescope more than a kilometre away, sailors noted the groups of letters. Then they looked up the meaning in their own code book.

Radio began to replace flag signals at the start of the 20th century. Nowadays, ships still use flags for decoration, but rarely to send messages.

The Egyptian code of the Rosetta Stone

The people of Ancient Egypt wrote in mysterious
pictures called **hieroglyphics**. What did they mean?
In 1799 French soldiers dug up a clue.
Near the Egyptian town of Rosetta they found
a big stone. It was carved with writing. At the bottom
was Greek, which some people could read.
Above, the same words appeared
in hieroglyphics. There were thousands
of different hieroglyphs: too many
to be an alphabet like our A
to Z of sound signs.
But there were not
enough for each
sign to stand for
just one word.

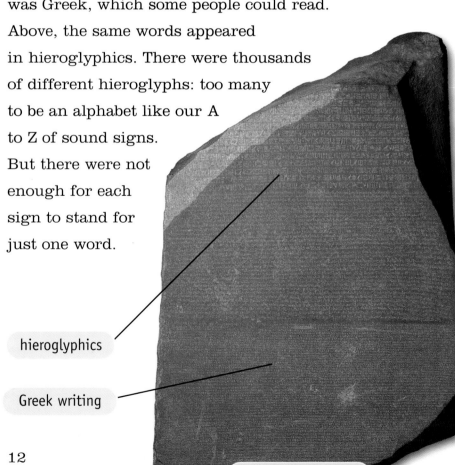

hieroglyphics

Greek writing

the Rosetta Stone

French language expert, Jean-François Champollion, noticed that the oval shapes, called cartouches, enclosed very few different hieroglyphs. He realised that this handful of signs stood for sounds, just like our letters! Overcome with excitement, he rushed to his brother's office, shouted "I've got it!" and fainted. Champollion later showed that every single one of the 5,000 hieroglyphs stood for an object or idea. The 24 alphabet sound signs were also used for objects. To write the letter "M", an Egyptian drew this sign:  But it could also mean an owl.

In hieroglyphic writing, a cartouche always contained the name of a king.

Champollion's work at last allowed us to understand the language and life of Ancient Egypt.

Egyptian scribes (writers) drew hieroglyphs with a pen made from reed.

Morse code

Samuel Morse

One of the most famous codes in history is Morse code. In 1822 an American painter called Samuel Morse had a brilliant idea. He realised that electricity could carry messages at lightning speed. His "electric telegraph" sent messages as bursts of electricity. As he hoped, the messages arrived without delay.

Morse wanted to use a book of codes, like the one sailors used. His assistant, Henry Vail, had a better idea. "Why not spell out letters with a code of short and long pulses?" Vail suggested one short pulse, a "dot", for the commonest letter, "E". Rarer letters used more pulses. The code for "Z" was two "dashes" (long pulses) and two dots: ▬ ▬ . .

This is the modern version of the code devised by Samuel Morse and Henry Vail.

van's code was named after his boss. In 1844, Morse code was buzzing down the very first telegraph wire. It connected the US capital, Washington DC, to Baltimore, 70 kilometres away. It was so successful that within four years, 20,000 kilometres of telegraph wires criss-crossed America.

Telegraph operators tapped out messages with an electrical switch called a "key".

Part 2: Making and breaking secret codes
Message on a belt

Two and a half thousand years ago, a Greek Spartan warrior dashed down a mountain. His belt was decorated with jumbled letters. His enemies ambushed him and searched him for a secret message, but found nothing, so they let him go.

At the end of his journey, the warrior's general took the belt. When he wrapped it round a special stick, the letters lined up.

"We have trapped the enemy ..." the hidden message said "... attack now!"

This way of keeping messages secret is called "scytale" (it rhymes with "Italy".) Scytales were the first secret codes and the Spartans were among the first to use them.

The Spartan people were fierce warriors. They ruled Greece for about 300 years from 650 BCE and the scytale code helped them defeat their enemies.

A paper strip is wrapped around a stick and the message is written on to it.

Unravelled from the stick, the message is now in code!

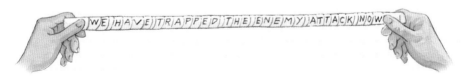

When the paper is wrapped round the same-size stick the message can be read (decoded).

Five hundred years after the Greeks kept their secrets with scytales, Romans ruled their country.

A Roman general called Julius Caesar knew the value of codes, so invented one himself. To keep his diary and letters secret from his enemies, he carefully jumbled up the letters.

He shifted each letter along the alphabet by the same amount. A three-letter shift turned A into D and F into I. So "Brutus is my friend" would read "Euxwxv lv pb iulhqg".

18

Caesar told all his friends the secret of the code so that they knew what to do when they received one of his alphabet puzzles. They shifted the letters back again to decode it and read the real message.

Caesar's code is one of the easiest to understand and is still used today as a simple code. The top line shows the alphabet. The bottom line shows the alphabet shifted three times.

A	B	C	D	E	F	G	H	I	J	K	L	M	N	O	P	Q	R	S	T	U	V	W	X	Y	Z
D	E	F	G	H	I	J	K	L	M	N	O	P	Q	R	S	T	U	V	W	X	Y	Z	A	B	C

Cracking the code

Caesar's code is very simple. If an enemy had captured Caesar's messenger, his coded words would not have been secret for long. A smart person could "crack" or "break" it – decode the message without knowing how Caesar had rearranged the letters. How? By counting the number of times a letter appears in a message.

We use some letters much more than others. E is the most common. We use J, K, Q, X and Z far less often. So by counting how many times a letter is used, you can soon see which one stands for E.

POST CARD

Nk dtz hfs wjfi
ymnx bwnynsl
dtz mfaj
hwfhpji ymj
htij

Emily Smith,
4 Rose Avenue,
Upton
Shropshire
SY5 9TQ

The writer of this postcard has used Caesar's code.

The most common letter used in this message is "J", so "J" stands for the most common letter in the English language: E. In this message, the alphabet has been shifted five times. If you apply this shift to every letter of the alphabet, you can read what it says.

The message reads: "If you can read this writing you have cracked the code".

Invisible ink

Another famous Roman kept his messages secret by making them vanish. Instead of dipping his pen in ink, Pliny used the clear liquid from a plant. When it dried, Pliny's message disappeared. He'd invented invisible ink.

Making Pliny's messages appear was easy – if you knew the trick. Gentle warming turned the letters brown.

Invisible ink can also be made from lemon juice or onion juice. Just like Pliny's "ink", the message will become visible again when the paper is warmed.

Invisible ink is used today.

Disguising the writing

Writing in invisible ink between the lines of an ordinary letter, or across the pale parts of a picture, makes the secret message harder to notice.

While in prison, Cuban leader Fidel Castro used lemon juice to write a whole book between the lines of letters he wrote to his half-sister.

Making Caesar smarter

Sliding every letter along the alphabet, as Caesar did, makes cracking a code easy, because as soon as you have guessed one letter right, you can guess them all.

Caesar's code has another weakness. Because there are just 26 letters in the alphabet, there are only 25 ways to shift them. A code-breaker who tried them out one by one would soon find a shift that worked.

A simple trick, invented in 1466 by the Italian architect and writer Leon Alberti, solved both these problems. He kept changing how much he slid the alphabet. For example, he might have shifted the first word by three letters, the next by six, the third by nine, and so on. Of course, whoever received his message had to also know this pattern.

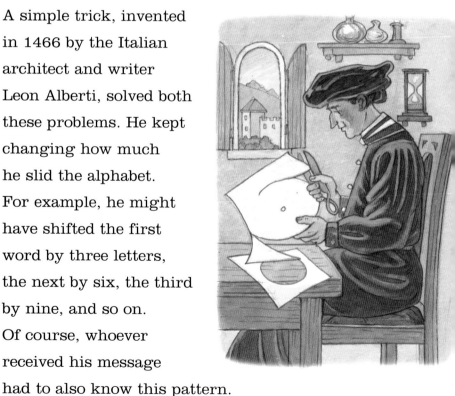

A code disc made this way of coding easier.

The two discs are loosely joined in the middle. The large disc is fixed, while the small one turns around.

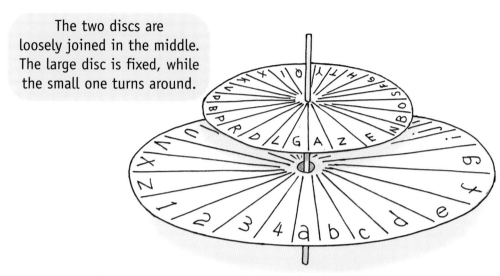

The larger disc shows letters in alphabetical order. The smaller disc shows the alphabet jumbled up. To code a message, Alberti found each letter on the inner ring and replaced it with the letter next to it on the outer ring. Rotating the inner ring changed the replacement letter. Alberti wrote in Latin, which lacked the letters J, U and W.

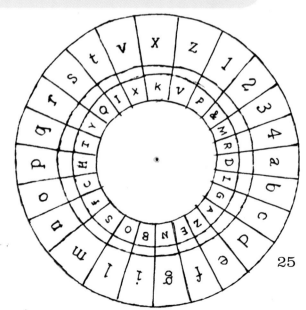

A secret grid from Italy

A century after Leon Alberti improved Caesar's code,
a smart Italian thought of a new way to hide his words.

Girolamo Cardano (1501–1576) invented a coding grid.
It was a simple piece of card with tiny windows cut in it.
He placed the grid on top of a sheet of writing paper.
He wrote words of his secret message through
each window. Then he removed the card, and filled
the gaps between
the words with
a longer message.
This gave no hint of
the secret hidden
inside it.

Cardano gave each
of his friends
copies of his grid,
so that they could
read the hidden
messages.

As well as inventing
codes, Girolamo Cardano was
an inventor and doctor.

Dear Kate
I am sorry I can't meet your
deadline. Fred phoned me saying I
had to drop extra work off at their
office. They wanted eight samples
done quickly. I'll have to do them
tonight. As usual my place is
too noisy to work easily but I'll
do my best.

Yours sincerely
Charlie

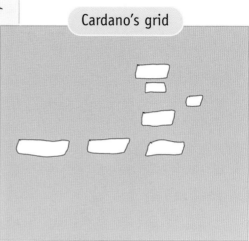

Cardano's grid

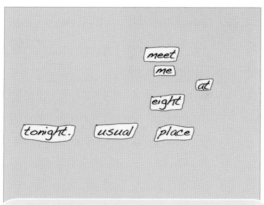

The enclosed message can be read
when the grid is placed over the letter.

The grid was rotated and/or flipped over before writing
through the windows. With just one grid, messages
could be written eight different ways.

Codes trap a queen

Queen Elizabeth I

While Cardano cut his little grids in Italy, coded letters were trapping a queen in England. Mary, Queen of Scots was held prisoner by her cousin Elizabeth I, England's queen. Elizabeth locked Mary up in 1568 because she was worried her cousin wanted to rule England.

After 18 years in prison, Mary proved her right. She was caught out in a plot to murder Elizabeth.

Mary, Queen of Scots

Mary's **gaoler** had stopped all her letters, so she was sending messages secretly to **allies** outside. She hid them in stoppers of beer barrels, and wrote them in code. Special signs replaced each letters (16th century writers rarely used the letters j, v and w). Here they are:

a b c d e f g h i k l m n o p q r s t u x y z
O ‡ ⋏ ⧻ ⍺ C θ ∞ ı ᕹ ⴺ ∥ ⌀ ▽ S ⋔ ƒ △ Ɛ ⊂ 7 8 9

However, Elizabeth's spies were reading Mary's mail. Mary used the same **substitution** every time and once the spies had worked this out, they could decode her letters. Mary was tried for her plotting and sentenced to death.

Writing on a fence

There are even simpler ways of jumbling messages. In America's Civil War, telegraph operators wrote whole words down the columns of a fence or grid, like this:

WE	CAMP	DIRECTION	AS	TO
WILL	20	WE	THE	ATTACK
BE	MILES	AGREED	ENEMY	OUR
MOVING	IN	AS	SEEMS	PRESENT
OUR	THE	SOON	READY	POSITION

Then they telegraphed the rows, so the message read:

"We camp direction as to will 20 we the attack be miles agreed enemy our moving in as seems present our the soon ready position."

Pigs in pens

Another simple code kept secret the messages of Civil
War prisoners. The prisoners drew a grid of lines,
like a noughts-and-crosses game. Then they wrote
the letters in the squares, like this:

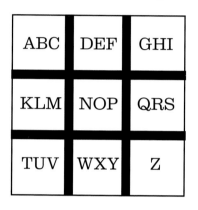

To write a letter in code, they
first drew an outline of the
square in which it appeared.
For example...

meant Q, R, S. Dots inside the shape picked out the
exact letter – for example, 1 for Q, 2 for R and 3 for S.

The grid and dots look a bit like fenced-in farm
animals, so this method of secret writing is sometimes
called the "pig-pen" code.

The Enigma code

In times of war, codes can keep battle plans secret
so that an enemy is surprised – and defeated.
However, *really* secure codes are slow and hard to use.
So as the First World War ended in 1918, German
engineer Arthur Scherbius invented a coding machine.
It made coding as easy as typing.

He called the machine Enigma. Code clerks worked it
from an ordinary keyboard. Pressing the keys sent
electricity through a row of discs. The position of each
disc decided which encoded letter lit up on a display.

the Enigma coding machine

Code clerks used key sheets like this one to prepare their machines.

What made the machine so clever was that each key press spun the discs, changing the code. So pressing "E" once might light up the letter "J". But pressing it again would light up a different letter. The number of different codes was huge. Even if everyone in the world tried one combination a second, it would take 75 years to crack the code.

When the Second World War began in 1939, German generals believed Enigma would keep their messages secret. They were wrong.

Breaking Enigma

Germany's enemies knew they would never break the Enigma code by hand. So they built machines to beat machines.

Poland's code experts were the first to make one of these code-cracking computers. A German **traitor** made their task easier. He handed over plans of the Enigma machines.

When the war began in 1939, the race to break Enigma moved to a top-secret base in England – Bletchley Park. Here Britain's most brilliant scientists studied hundreds of coded German messages daily. They built bigger, better computers, called bombes.

a working replica of a bombe machine

They were helped by the German code clerks! The clerks' mistakes and lazy shortcuts provided vital clues to Enigma. Captured code books also helped Bletchley Park experts guess how clerks used the machines. Repeated words in messages, known as "cribs", gave away more of Enigma's secrets.

By 1942 Bletchley Park was regularly decoding Enigma messages. Their amazing work saved countless lives. It may have cut short the war by two years.

Experts at Bletchley Park decoding German codes.

Navajo code talkers

Machines such as Enigma turned writing into code, but they didn't work with speech. A general who bellowed orders into a radio could be sure the enemy would hear them.

In 1942, United States troops began fighting to control the Pacific Ocean. They needed radios to talk to each other. But they guessed that their Japanese enemies had radio operators who understood English.

They solved the problem by training Navajo radio operators. Navajo are Native American people. They speak their own unique language. None of the enemy understood it.

Navajo radio operators using their own language to baffle the enemy.

Nicknamed "Windtalkers", the Navajo added extra secrecy. They used codes for words their language lacked. Submarines were unknown on the American plains where they lived, so they called them "iron fish". In the same way, a fighter plane became a "hummingbird", a battleship was a "whale" and a grenade was a "potato".

Soldiers used this clever idea again at the end of the 20th century. The British army employed Welsh-speaking radio operators while fighting in Bosnia.

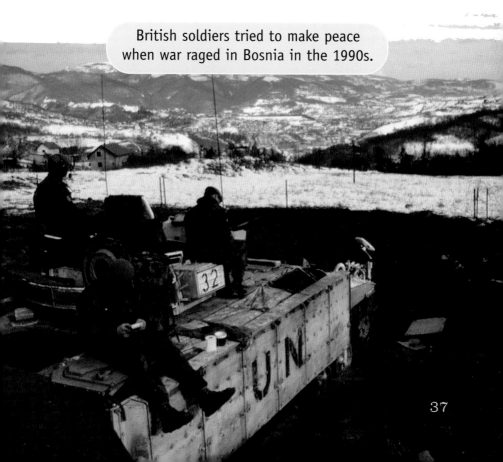

British soldiers tried to make peace when war raged in Bosnia in the 1990s.

Cold War spies

When the Second World War ended in 1945, peace did not return. Russia and the USA remained enemies. People called their rivalry the Cold War. The two nations spied on each other. Their secret agents used unbreakable codes.

They made them with "one-time pads" of printed number grids and Caesar's code. They took the first letter of a message and shifted it along the alphabet as Caesar did. The first number in the grid showed how far to shift the first letter. The second number showed how far to shift the second letter ... and so on.

What made the code so secret was that spies used each grid only once. To exchange messages, two spies had to have identical grids. But even if an enemy captured a grid, they would understand just one message. The grid was no help for messages that followed.

Part 3: Unbroken codes and forgotten languages

The biggest code mysteries of all are ancient languages. Like hieroglyphics three centuries ago, they have beaten even the cleverest people.

Proto-Elamite

Five thousand years ago, in the region we now call Iraq, Elamite people wrote by pressing lines into mud blocks. Only a little of this Proto-Elamite script has been decoded. Most signs are still a mystery.

The Etruscan language

Etruscan people lived in
what we now know as Italy.
The letters they used looked like
the Greek alphabet. However,
the words they spelt out were
unlike any words from Greece –
or anywhere else. The last person
to understand Etruscan died
nearly 2,000 years ago.

41

Zapotec script

Around 2,500 years ago the Zapotec people of southern Mexico wrote with picture-signs scratched on stones. The lines of writing run downwards and the few signs we can read are

about dates and calendars. The rest are a mystery.

Rongorongo

People, fish and animals dance through the Rongorongo writing of Easter Island in the Pacific Ocean. But what is the meaning of these signs, which are all carved on driftwood? We have no idea, because the last person who could read them died nearly 150 years ago. What we *do* know is that reading them was very different from reading English. You start at the bottom left, then turn the page upside-down each time you reach the end of a line.

These puzzles have baffled everyone until now. This does not mean they cannot be solved. One day, someone who studies them will, like Champollion, decode a single word. Then another and one more, until the puzzle is unlocked. Could you be the one to do it?

Glossary

allies   a group of people or countries who work together

BCE   before the Common Era: before the birth of Christ

ciphers   written codes

gaoler   someone who guards a prisoner

hieroglyphics   a writing system that uses symbols or pictures for objects, concepts, or sounds

Middle Ages   the name given to the time between the 5th century and the 15th century

plumes   columns of smoke that are shaped like feathers

spies   people who get secret information from another person or country

substitution   replacing one thing with another

traitor   a person guilty of betraying their country, friends or beliefs

Index

Different types of code

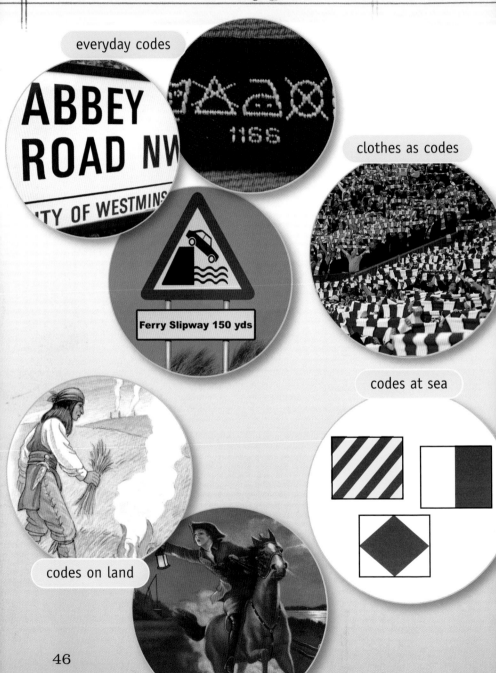

everyday codes

clothes as codes

Ferry Slipway 150 yds

codes at sea

codes on land

written codes

electric codes

number codes

invisible codes

unsolved!

47

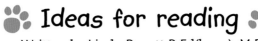

Ideas for reading

Written by Linda Pagett B.Ed(hons), M.Ed
Lecturer and Educational Consultant

Learning objectives: use knowledge of different organisational features of texts to find information effectively; listen to a speaker; make notes and use to develop role play; convey detailed information coherently for listeners

Curriculum links: Mathematics; Citizenship: Taking part – developing skills of communication and participation

Interest words: spies, codes, ciphers, warchalking, Middle Ages, plumes, hieroglyphics, Rosetta Stone, cartouches, Morse code, scytale code, Cardano's grid, allies, gaoler, Enigma code

Resources: writing materials

Getting started

This book may be read over two or more guided reading sessions.

- Discuss codes with the children, finding out what they already know about them, *When are codes likely to be used?*

- Together, begin to make a list of different types of code and the purpose of them, e.g. *texting for speed; postcodes to help find addresses.*

- Together, look at the front and back covers of the book. Help the children to infer information from the pictures on the cover, e.g. *What clues are there to help us find out what time this is? What country could it be?*

- Read the blurb and ask children what kind of features might be useful in an information book, e.g. *diagrams, captions, photos, glossary.*

Reading and responding

- Read the contents page together. Agree the best way to read an information book. Do children need to read each chapter in order, or can they dip in?